larger than life:
JOE NAMATH

Author

Val Albrecht

Photography

Ron Koch
Bruce Curtis

 **RAINTREE EDITIONS**

Published by   **Raintree Editions**
A Division of Raintree Publishers Limited
Milwaukee, Wisconsin 53203

Distributed by   Childrens Press
1224 West Van Buren Street
Chicago, Illinois 60607

Library of Congress Cataloging in Publication Data

Albrecht, Val K.
  Larger than life.

  SUMMARY: A biography of the football player who
rose to fame as quarterback for the New York Jets.
  1. Namath, Joe Willie, 1943-   —Juvenile literature.
2. Football—Juvenile literature. [1. Namath, Joe Willie,
1943-   2. Football—Biography]
I. Koch, Ron . II. Curtis, Bruce. III. Title.
GV939.N28A62   796.33'2'0924 [B] [92]   75-42313
ISBN 0-8172-0113-0
ISBN 0-8172-0112-2 lib. bdg.

Contents

Instant Fame

Probably no other football player in the history of the game is as famous as Joe Willie Namath.

Fans of every team in the country have their favorite players, but none is as widely-known as the star quarterback for the New York Jets.

Namath's fame stems from much more than his pinpoint passing ability on the gridiron. He has become a genuine celebrity. A one-of-a-kind person — admired or scorned, but never forgotten.

He's seen on national television in commercials and guest appearances. His name is used to sell everything from sport shirts to games. He's written two books. He's appeared in three movies. He's active in charity work.

And all the time, he's Joe Namath. Six-feet-two-inches tall, 200 pounds, green eyes, dark hair, mod dress. Part hero, part rascal, part zany. Totally serious about his playing, but having fun at it, too. Always himself — just as comfortable in a posh restaurant as he is in the Jets' locker room.

His every move is reported in the sports pages of newspapers, the gossip columns, the movie magazines, radio, television. People know about his white football shoes, his injuries, his friends, his businesses, his long hair,

his contracts, his family.

In fact, so much has been reported about Joe that it is hard to separate the real from the unreal, the person from the publicity, the man from the myth.

This much, however, is very real: After four years as a quarterback at Alabama University, Namath skyrocketed into the headlines by signing with the Jets as the highest-paid rookie of all time. It was no accident. Conditions in national football were right for the creation of a superstar, and jaunty Namath was a natural for the role.

Football in America started in 1869 as a college sport. Gradually it spread to high schools and clubs such as the YMCA. By 1895, the sport had become so popular that professional teams were formed — mostly so that a fine player's training wouldn't be wasted after he left high school.

In 1920, the American Professional Football League was formed. This organization later became the National Football League. The league established teams and set all the rules.

Soon, football was a national pastime and preoccupation. People crowded to the games to cheer on their teams. They followed accounts of the action in newspapers. When radio found its way onto the American scene, play-by-play descriptions of the games were broadcast to bring even more of the excitement to even more people.

Then along came television. Suddenly people could see and hear the games in their own living rooms.

Advertisers soon realized that a lot of people were hooked on the game. They began to pay big money to get their ads aired during football broadcasts.

Lamar Hunt, a Texas millionaire, saw that there was a fortune to be made in football. So he founded the American Football League to rival the NFL.

The New York Titans was one of the eight original AFL

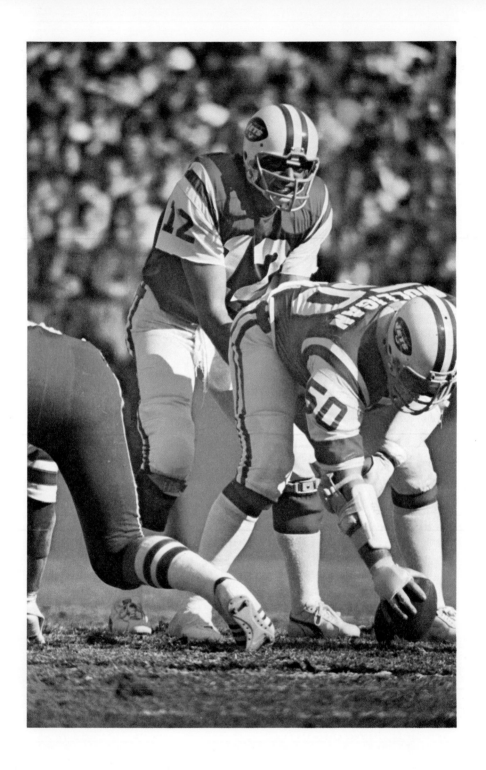

teams. It had a tough time. The team had to fight for ticket sales with the established New York Giants of the NFL. It was bothered by poor management. Morale among the players was low. For awhile, the future looked bleak.

But then the Titans were taken over by a group headed by David A. ("Sonny") Werblin. Werblin loved football — but he *knew* show business. He had been head of the Music Corporation of America, an entertainment talent agency that handled clients such as Ed Sullivan, Jackie Gleason, Andy Williams, and many other top stars.

Werblin was sure he could change the losing image of the Titans with some showmanship. He changed the team's name to the Jets, which sounded more alive and modern. He moved the games from the old Polo Grounds to Shea Stadium, which was easier to reach from anywhere in the New York area.

And he signed Joe Namath as the highest-paid rookie ever — for a $427,000 bonus contract.

The press, always eager for something new in sports, went wild! Nearly half a million dollars for a quarterback fresh out of the university! Unheard of!

But Werblin knew that the signing probably gave the Jets over a million dollars worth of free publicity. And he hoped that Joe would become a central figure who would eventually draw the players together into a winning team.

After sorting out all the rumors, guesses, comments, and criticism about the signing, one fact was eventually proven. Werblin had made a good investment in Namath.

"I don't know if anyone can define what makes a star," Werblin has said. "Whatever it is, Namath has it. He walks into a room and suddenly it's exciting. He's young, eager, and has a certain style all his own. He does his own thing and does it well."

Superstar. Super Jet.

A Long Way From Beaver Falls

Joe Namath was a junior superstar in Beaver Falls, Pennsylvania, where he was born and raised. His three older brothers started him early on baseball, basketball, and football.

Joe was crazy about sports. He quit being an altar boy because it cut into his gym time before regular school hours. Somehow, he and his friends managed to use the gym even on Sundays, when it was locked.

Breaking into the gym was only one of Joe's pastimes. "I wasn't exactly a saint as a kid," he admits. Some of his throwing practice was done with rocks, using the windows of a local laundry as a target. He also admits to truancy, hustling, and a number of other pranks that kept him in hot water with his brothers and parents.

Pool was one of Joe's specialties. He usually won. He also liked golf and fishing. But he went hunting only once. He saw a small animal die, and never hunted again.

"I didn't study much in school because sports were much more fun," Joe says. "Cash was also fun. I used to sell lemonade at a factory with my sister Rita—using my mother's lemons, of course. When I was old enough, Wednesdays were out as far as school was concerned. I could make $6 caddying on the golf course, and that sure beat an afternoon at the books."

Joe's grandparents came from Hungary in 1921. They settled in Beaver Falls, where work was available in the steel mill. Joe's father, John Namath, worked in the mill, too. It was hot, loud, and very hard work. He didn't like it much. But he needed the money so he could give his children good educations. He was determined that they would have somthing better than he had.

John Namath often turned to sports as a break from the long hours he spent in the mill. Joe and his brothers got their love of sports from their father.

Joe's parents were divorced when he was 12. He lived with his mother.

"My mother sure worked hard to raise me the right way," Joe says. "When I was a kid, to help out with money, she had a job as a maid in Patterson Heights, the richer section of town. Now she lives there. . . . Anyway, she had her hands full with the bunch of us. She's a real lady. I guess you could say we have a mutual admiration society going. She still watches every game I play and is the only person I know who prays to a separate offensive and defensive saint."

Joe's brother Frank was a kind of substitute father after his parents separated. "I remember once when I was still in high school Frank got wind of the fact that I'd been in a bar. It had really been for just a minute to pick up a friend, but my brother was boiling mad! He chased me on foot and in our cars, and then — just before I sure thought he was going to clobber me — he stopped to hear me out. When I told him what really happened he calmed down. Guess he was just being really concerned about my starting any bad habits."

Even now, Namath doesn't lie . . . except to stretch things now and then with girls. He'll either tell the straight truth, or use an obvious put-on with people. Sometimes his listeners can't tell the difference. Many reporters have taken his jokes as fact, which accounts for some of the strange things printed and said about his career and private life.

By the time Joe got to high school, he was a pretty good football player. But he sat out his freshman year because he was too small to make the regular team. "I moaned plenty," he says, "but the coach was firm. He encouraged me to train, and taught me a lot in practice even though I warmed the bench during the games."

Joe finally did make the team, and by his junior year he was a real star. When the football season was over, he'd switch to basketball and baseball. He was a star in those sports, too. "Maybe that was because as a kid we ran around in gangs and we had enough rock fights to develop my throwing arm," he says.

It also was in high school that Joe began living his own style. He was off-beat, inventive, and forever striving to be the best he could be in sports.

At one basketball game, he took the court 15 minutes before the scheduled start and gave a dribbling/throwing exhibition that had the crowd cheering. When the team photograph was made, he wouldn't take off his dark glasses. He thought they had class.

Joe and his friends had a standing joke. They'd look solemnly in the mirror and quip, "I can't wait until tomorrow 'cause I get better looking every day." That joking boast eventually became the title of Joe's first book.

Joe could have had a pro basketball contract after graduation from high school. And a baseball team offered him $20,000 to join. But John Namath convinced his son that a good university education was far more valuable to his future than an immediate slot in pro basketball or baseball.

"Luckily," says Joe, "I had over 50 football scholarships offered, mostly because our school team had performed so

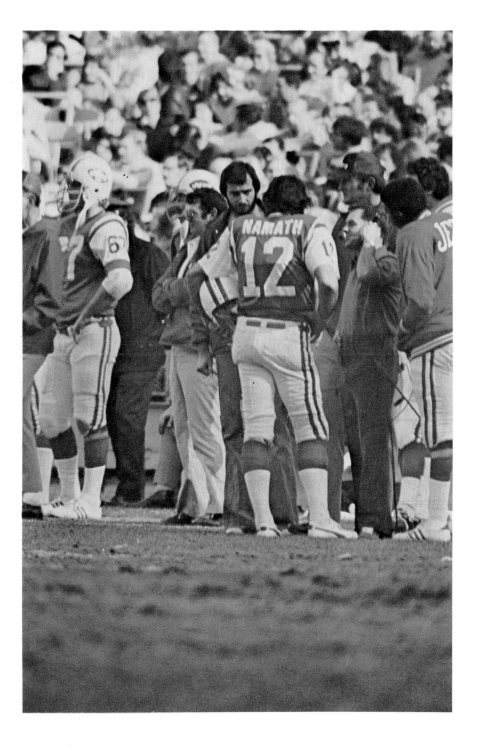

great." Joe may claim luck for the offers, but his high school records show that he had superior throwing and running skills. He was a player any school would value.

It took Joe awhile to sort out the offers.

"I heard that a guy from Michigan came to talk to me about the university there. At the time I think I was lounging on top of my car when he was looking for me. I never did meet him, so I guess he took just one look and decided I wouldn't belong in his state.

"Then I had an offer from Notre Dame. When I found out it was an all-male school, I figured it wasn't the place for me.

"Finally I decided I wanted to play down south . . . Maryland, where I had a buddy. You can tell my geography wasn't so hot. Anyway, my college boards weren't so hot either. The first time I took the Maryland exam I didn't pass. The second time I missed by about ten points. That crossed me out at Maryland."

There's a story, possibly true, that after Joe failed the Maryland entrance exam, the school's coach was afraid he might play with Penn State. The Penn State team was a tough one, one of the strongest on Maryland's upcoming schedule. With Namath playing, it would be even harder to beat.

So, the story goes, Maryland officials phoned Alabama coach Paul ("Bear") Bryant. They told him about Joe's great playing. Alabama added its offer to the long string of possible scholarships.

After considerable discussion with his high school coach, his family, and friends, Joe decided that he would play in a real southern state. Along with excellent coaching, the Alabama scholarship covered full tuition and fees, room and board, and $15 a month for laundry fees. Not exactly the lavish living that Namath would make later.

Other schools had made better offers, including salaries

and cars, but Namath played things straight. He now thinks it was one of the better decisions of his life.

At first Joe was homesick, but then he met Ray Abruzzese, who also was from Pennsylvania. The two hit it off at once and became good friends. The friendship — like most of those Joe makes — has lasted to this day. They even shared a New York apartment and a business for a while.

Joe's lawyer, Jimmy Walsh, also was an Alabama student. So was Mike Bite, who is his business advisor. They formed a group that is still close.

Joe's football career at Alabama was full of ups and downs. Joe was suspended late in his third year because he was seen taking a drink. "Coach Bryant didn't want to do it, but I couldn't lie to him. He had no other choice but to enforce the rules. Maybe I learned as much from the punishment as I did from playing."

When Namath was a sophomore, Alabama was ranked number one in the college ratings — until they lost to Georgia Tech. In his senior year, he really wanted to beat Georgia Tech and re-establish Alabama as the top team in the country.

But Joe's knee was injured. Coach Bryant didn't want to use him unless it was absolutely necessary. In the last minutes of the first quarter there was still no score. Then Namath was sent in. "I was lousy. One pass knocked down, another was short. Then I connected with Dave Ray, a flanker, who carried into the end zone for a 7-0 lead."

By the end of that game, Joe had completed four passes of eight attempts, racking up 104 yards and a touchdown. Alabama won, 24-7.

Later that year, Alabama was invited to play in the Orange Bowl. Again, Joe's bad knee made it doubtful if he could play. The trainer used ice packs to ease the pain and bring down the swelling. That and Namath's determination to

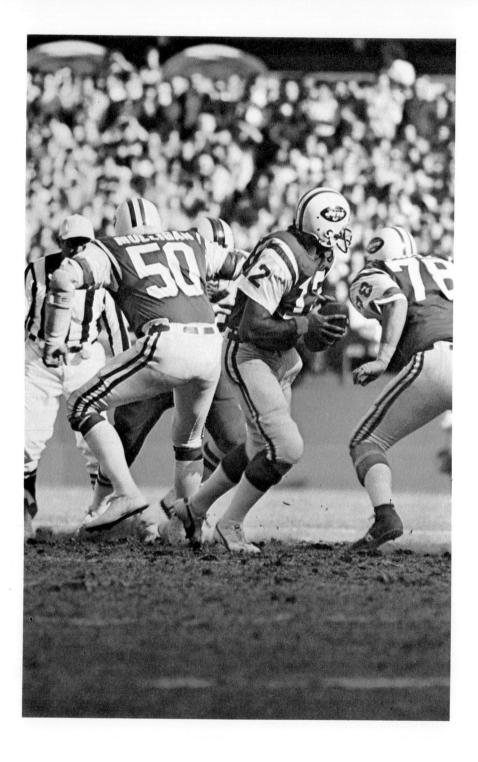

get in the game overcame any reservation Bryant may have had about using him.

When the score against Texas in the Bowl game was 14-0, Namath zoomed onto the field. His leg may have been bad, but his passing was spectacular. In the last minutes of the game, he carried the ball and lunged over the goal line. Joe still claims that he scored. The officials didn't think so. Alabama lost, 21-17. A real heartbreaker.

Sonny Werblin of the New York Jets was in the stands that day. He didn't mind that Alabama lost. He was looking at Namath. "Fabulous, fabulous!" he said. He was right.

Jets' Superbomb?

The Alabama veteran quarterback was just a rookie when he joined the Jets. Sonny Werblin showed him off to New York, and Namath enjoyed all the attention. Suddenly, he was a star. Everyone was talking about the $427,000 player. He did his best to live up to the reputation created for him by all the publicity.

He tooled around town in the big Lincoln Continental that was part of his contract. He took a neat bachelor's apartment with his old friend, Ray Abruzzese, for a reported $400 a month. He dated beautiful women and was seen in the better nightspots around New York. He really earned his nickname, "Broadway Joe."

Werblin took him to the races and the opera, to fine restaurants and swank parties, to the theater and the golf course. Showmanship paid off. It almost seemed as if every line written about the cool rookie from Beaver Falls sold another ticket to a game. The Jets' financial picture brightened. The future looked sunny.

However, all was not well. Joe's friendship with the team's owner did not endear him to his teammates. Players who had signed earlier, some with the original Titans, were naturally resentful of Namath's contract. Some remembered the days when they weren't sure they'd get paid at all, let alone paid as handsomely as the newcomer.

Joe's contract apparently covered his first four years of salary at about $25,000 a season, the lawyer's fee, a car (the Lincoln), and a $200,000 bonus to be paid over a period of years. Scouting salaries for his two brothers and his brother-in-law were also included.

Small wonder that the rest of the team did a not-so-slow boil. Joe himself hit it on the head. "Who likes a rich rookie?"

Then, too, Namath's put-ons and jaunty style put off the others. Even Coach Weeb Ewbank was cautious with the newcomer until he learned more about Joe's talents. Joe's first pro games were spent manning the phones, relaying coaching comments from the spotters to the field.

In that first year, Namath was never really accepted by the team. The Jets were a group of single players, never an effective, well-functioning unit.

But then the players got together for a gripe session. No coaches or owners were allowed at the meeting. Namath took the opportunity to stand up and tell the others how he felt. He said he knew how they must feel, and that he didn't much blame them. "Don't judge me by the money," he said. "Judge me on how I play ball. If I do something wrong, say so. I'll do the best I know how. I came here to be on the team and I hope we'll make it—together."

Namath meant every word. He wanted to play football more than anything else.

Joe suffered a painful injury in his last year at Alabama and had knee surgery before coming to the Jets' training camp. After the operation he had to wear an aluminum knee brace. Some of the other players griped when Joe was excused from running laps around the field. But he actually converted the brace problem into one of his strongest assets.

By changing his style to compensate for the brace, Joe improved his throwing considerably. He couldn't drop back to pass with the crossover step used by most quarterbacks on taking the snap. Instead, he learned to take three quick steps straight back, lean on his good left leg, and zip off a pass with almost unbelievable speed.

His fast set-up meant fewer sacks — though he's suffered his share — but during his pro career he never could be a real running quarterback.

At first, Joe's playing was not at all consistent. Some of his passes were deadly accurate — and others were wildly off the mark. But steadily he improved. He disciplined himself to learn more than 700 plays. He learned to read the defense in a split second, and to spot an open receiver without any evident change in movement from the time of taking the snap to winging the ball.

He learned, in other words, to play masterful pro ball, and became a respected team leader. And he did it his own way, without giving up the high lifestyle that attracted so much attention.

By his own admission, he loved "booze, broads, and betting." The very fact that he didn't hesitate to say so — that he was himself always — made headlines. He gained a reputation as a heavy drinker, a girl chaser, and a gambler. Seldom did he bother to correct the impressions created by his own flip comments.

Most of his teammates eventually realized that the press accounts were exaggerated. Broadway Joe may have been a swinger, but he never let anything interfere with his playing.

One night Joe broke training. The incident was blown all out of proportion. There were tales that he habitually broke the rules, or just made up his own. Everyone who repeated the story added his own details, until Joe's name was mud.

According to Namath's own version, he only broke training once. He was troubled by family problems. Feeling that he really needed some time out of camp to be alone and

think things through, he asked Coach Ewbank for permission to have a night off in New York. The coach refused, mostly because Namath was too proud to tell him the real reason for his request.

So he went "absent without leave" and had a night on the town to relieve the tension he was under. The next morning he returned to camp. The fine was $500. He paid it without a murmur. Practice went on as usual.

Joe's lifestyle has often caused him trouble. But once it nearly caused him to resign from football.

Like most football players who know that their playing careers won't last a lifetime, Joe invested money in businesses that would provide future income. But in his typical Namath way, he wanted his businesses to be fun.

Namath and two close friends went into partnership and opened the Bachelors III, a New York nightclub. It was a place for the young to congregate; a place where Joe and his friends could meet and entertain other buddies, and make some money while enjoying the whole thing.

Commissioner of Football Pete Rozelle felt that the Bachelors III was an unfit business; that it did not conform to the standards set for professional players.

Rozelle had been told that the Bachelors III was a hangout for gamblers. He issued an order to Namath — sell or resign from football.

Namath was enraged. He hated lies. He hated hypocrites. It was general knowledge that many other players had interests in restaurants. And Joe knew that many players placed bets, though usually not on football games. Weren't they "gamblers"? Besides, how could he keep gamblers out of his club? It was a public place of business, and under the laws of the city he had no control over who could enter. He couldn't understand why he was being singled out.

His first impulse was to resign. Then the love of football and loyalty to his teammates changed his mind.

He would sell.

No, he would resign. He had to be true to his own principles.

He'd sell. He'd resign.

Perhaps the clash over the Bachelors III was really a coverup; an attempt to ease Namath out of pro ball because of his freewheeling lifestyle. Perhaps Rozelle was genuinely concerned about the reports of "shady associates" and feared the possible consequences for the whole league. Whatever the reason, Joe was faced with a real dilemma.

Finally Namath called a press conference for 10 o'clock in the morning — an uncivilized hour for a night person like Joe. He planned to meet with reporters in the questionable club and make his decision known.

Dressed in jeans and a tuxedo shirt, with a paper cup of coffee in hand, he faced the press. Actually, almost to the last minute, it is doubtful that he knew himself exactly what he intended to do.

Like the cavalry arriving to save the wagon train in a western movie, Namath's attorneys and advisors were able to negotiate a last-minute compromise. It was agreed with Commissioner Rozelle that Joe would sell out his share of the club to his partners. The "bad boy quarterback" stayed with the Jets to mature and improve. And set new records.

Jets' Superstar

Gradually the other Jets began to see Joe Namath as a person and an excellent player, not just a dollar sign. His playing and snap judgments on the field become more and more vital to the team's success.

Joe continued to work on his style. He was determined to be more than good — he wanted to be best. He ignored the repeated injuries to his legs as much as he could. Even when his legs were in bad shape, his rifle-like passing continued to improve.

Finally he earned the full cooperation and support of his fellow players. To a man, the offensive team rallied to protect their quarterback with the fragile legs.

If ever a man worked for and deserved the description "living legend," it was Joe Namath of the Jets. Howard Cosell, commenting on a 1975 Jets' game on television, summed things up nicely. "The Jets are a different team with Namath on it," he said.

On the field, Joe's movements are smooth. Everything he does looks easy — mostly because of hard, constant practice.

Backed by outstanding teamwork, he can call a play in the huddle, read a shift in the defense at the line of scrimmage, and change the call immediately to a more effective play. The team responds. In an instant, every player switches gears to execute the new play.

It all looks so easy. It all costs so much in time, study, memorization, discipline, and practice, practice, practice.

Namath hates hard work. To endure the grind week after week, he sure must love football.

In 1968, the Jets showed Joe just how much they had come to respect him. "I can't ever remember being so happy before," Joe says. "Clive Rush, one of our coaches, came up to me to offer his congratulations. I didn't know what I'd done. Then he told me I'd been elected captain of the offensive team. Those guys will probably never know how much it meant to me."

Joe would be chosen captain of the offensive team again in 1969, 1970, and 1972. He would be voted the team's Most Valuable Player in 1968, 1969, and 1974. He would receive other honors. He would make the AFL All-Star team in 1965, 1967, 1968, and 1969, and the American Football Conference All-Star team in 1972. He'd be named a member of the All-Time All-AFL Squad selected by the Pro Football Hall of Fame.

Joe was sidelined with injuries in 1970, 1971, and 1973. But somehow, he always managed to come back. In 1972, he passed for more yards than anyone in football, and tied for the NFL lead with 19 touchdowns. He won All-Pro honors and was selected for the All-Pro Bowl, although he couldn't play in the game because of an ankle injury. He also became the third quarterback in history, following George Blanda and Sonny Jurgensen, to have two 400-yard games in one year.

Nineteen seventy-four was another good year. After a bad season opening, the Jets finished with six straight wins. By this time, Weeb Ewbank had been replaced by a new coach, Charlie Winner. Winner called Namath "a most efficient quarterback." High praise from a tough coach.

During the '74 winning streak, Joe completed 85 of 147 passes for 1,196 yards and 11 touchdowns. Of his last 80 passes over three and a half games that year, he had no interceptions at all. His total yardage for the season was 2,616, second best in the league.

There have been many exciting games in the Namath career. The game against the Baltimore Colts, when he and opposing quarterback Johnny Unitas combined to gain just under half a mile in passing, must be counted among the most outstanding.

But most reporters and fans agree that the 1969 Super Bowl was the ultimate. The Jets were playing the Colts. Professional oddsmakers put the Jets as the 21-point underdogs, even though they were league champions with an 11-3 record. Baltimore had won its title with a 13-1 record.

After defeating the Oakland Raiders for the league championship, the Jets turned their attention to the Colts. They studied films of the Colts' previous games. Reviewing movies of opposing teams' games is required of all team members. But Namath takes it so seriously that he often has films run over and over until he can spot weak places in the defense that can be turned to his advantage.

After watching the Colts' films, Joe's only fear was that they might change their defense. "Teams playing the Colts before just didn't know how to handle their blitz," he said. "I could see the patterns leaving their middle open, and I knew I could pass to our wide receivers even if I got hit myself."

Namath actually hoped that the Colts would try their blitz on the Jets.

The Jets went to Fort Lauderdale for pre-Bowl practice. Joe was under constant supervision of the team doctor, who

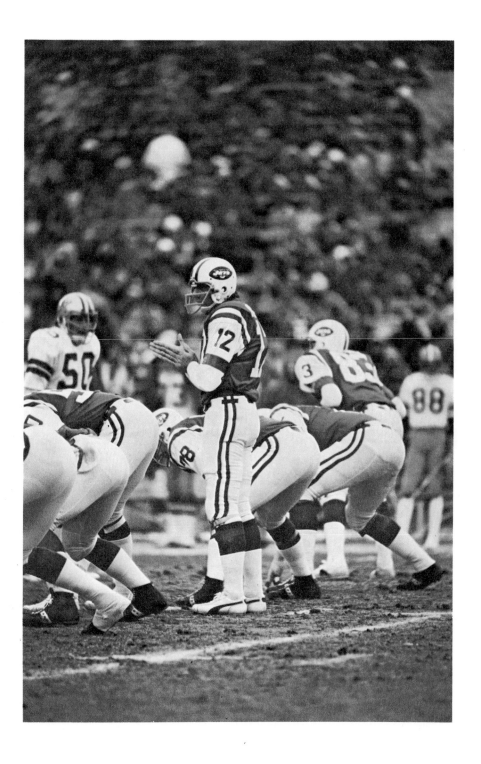

drained fluid from his bad knee and gave him painkillers when necessary.

Three days before the game, Joe went down to Miami Springs Villa, where he received an Outstanding Player award from the Touchdown Club. During his acceptance speech, Joe Namath — superconfident, superbrash, superstar — made a flat prediction. "I guarantee that the Jets will win the Super Bowl," he said.

In spite of the odds, the Colts' outstanding record, Unitas' brilliance, the roster of great players, Namath really believed the Jets would win. He was sure, and he made his teammates sure, too. They went into the game with great morale, faith in their quarterback, and a certainty of winning.

The game was played on January 12 in the Orange Bowl Stadium at Miami. It was an overcast day with a temperature in the low 70s. Millions of Americans watched at home along with the 75,000 spectators who packed the stands.

Each player on the winning team would receive $15,000; $7,500 each to the losers. That's a lot of money, but this particular game was played for far higher stakes.

On the Jet offense, Namath made 17 of 28 passes for a total yardage of 206. The Colts' quarterback Morrall completed 6 of 17 passes for 71 yards with three interceptions; Unitas 11 of 24 for 110 yards with one interception. Unitas played only in the fourth quarter, and managed the team's only score, a one-yard scramble by Hill.

Namath was steady throughout, and Matt Snell carried 30 times for 121 yards. The Jets' defense intercepted Morrall three times in the first half, effectively stopping Baltimore's offense.

The Jets won the game, 16-7, just as Joe said they would. And Joe was voted the game's Most Valuable Player. But there was something else; something more important. For the first time, an AFL team had taken the Super Bowl.

It was a great day for Joe Namath of the New York Jets.

The Price

Joe Namath's mother, Rose Szolnoki, says no amount of money could ever compensate for the constant pain her son endures as a result of his athletic career. It is hard for him to walk. Hard to sit without sprawling. Harder still to play ball.

As a youngster, Joe had two attacks of severe leg pain. The first time, he ran a high fever and polio was suspected. Then his temperature dropped and the pain let up. He was fine until the following spring. The pain began again. He was hospitalized for three weeks.

No real cause for the childhood illness was ever found. Exercise seemed to help — and he got plenty of that through school and into the pros.

During his senior year at Alabama, he injured his right leg. "I still think it was because I didn't use white tape around my shoes, and I wore a T-shirt that day." Namath remains very superstitious about those two ideas. He still wears white shoes on the field (only now the Jets' management has them made specially for him). And there's never an undershirt beneath the famous number 12 jersey.

Just 23 days after signing his first contract with the Jets in 1965, Joe had surgery to correct the damage to his right leg. It continued to hurt, though, and he tended to rely too

U.S. 1991153

much on his left leg for balance and bracing when passing. As a result, he developed bursitis in that leg. This is a painful inflammation in the joints and tendons. The ailment hampered most of his running plays.

That first operation, and all the others to follow, was performed by the team surgeon, Dr. James Nicholas. Nicholas has become a kind of friendly enemy to Namath. He's the one who injects the long needles to extract fluid from Joe's kneecap or administer medication to curb the pain.

Joe wears a special aluminum brace designed by inventor Ignatius Castiglia, a polio victim. The brace weighs less than two pounds and allows support to be coupled with leg mobility.

Over the years, Joe has had four major leg operations. He has suffered numerous other injuries, including a shoulder separation and a broken wrist.

Joe seems to have had more than his share of trouble, but he tends to shrug it off. After all, he says, there isn't a pro football player worth his salt who hasn't suffered an injury at some time during his career.

"I could feel pretty sorry for myself, I guess," Joe says. "Maybe I would if I hadn't been through some military hospitals in Japan, Okinawa, and Hawaii. That was right after the Super Bowl. You see those guys who have really suffered, lost arms and legs, and you realize fast how small your own problems are."

Joe's mother is probably right. No money can make up for the pain that will be with him the rest of his life. Of all the things written and said about Joe, accounts of his fragile legs are probably closest to the truth.

But legs are the subject Joe Namath likes least to discuss. He doesn't look for sympathy.

For Namath, pain is the price of playing football. He pays it. That's a reality.

What Now, Joe?

Nineteen seventy-five was a year of speculation about the future of the Jets' star quarterback. Would he resign? Would he switch to the new World Football League? Would injury strike again and force his retirement?

New opinions and theories seemed to pop up every day. But then, at last, Joe Namath signed a $400,000-plus contract to play another two years with the New York Jets.

After the blazing six-game winning streak at the end of the 1974 season, '75 was less than spectacular. Namath's passing was, as usual, superb for the most part. "When I was good, I was very, very good," Joe says. "When I was bad, I was lousy."

He escaped major injury. The team didn't. The win-lose record was dismal — 11 losses in a 14-game schedule. The only star was fullback John Riggins, who racked up a season total of 1,003 yards, making him the only Jet ever to go beyond the 1,000-yard mark.

So what now, Joe Namath?

"I have a contract for the next season and I intend to honor it," he said in a newspaper interview.

But no football career is long compared with other professions. Younger players constantly compete for the

slots of the older veterans. Some day, injury or age will make Namath leave football for another field. It's just a matter of time.

Fortunately, Namath finds other things fun, too. And profitable. He doesn't believe in worrying, not about himself at least, and is content to take life as it comes.

Part of his uniqueness is that he is always himself. No pretenses. Somehow, his mix of brashness and competence is appealing. The contradictions in his personality may make him difficult to understand, but they certainly make him interesting. The problem of trying to figure him out is made harder because he often won't explain the things that are said about him. His continual wisecracking multiplies the misunderstandings.

Being himself means that Joe's zany a lot of the time. What kind of person would grow a Fu Manchu mustache, treading dangerously close to breaking the league rules on grooming, and then make a grand gesture of shaving it off for a television commercial?

What other pro football player would display a pair of rickety legs on national television in a panty hose commercial?

Namath thought it was fun. He made three movies for the same reason . . . and learned a lot about acting in the process. He had a small part in *Norwood,* with Glen Campbell. He also appeared in *The Last Rebel* and *C.C. and Company,* in which he did a very creditable acting job.

He has had his own TV special, *The Joe Namath Show,* and has appeared on a number of other programs, including the Sonny and Cher show, and many of the Dean Martin comedy roasts.

Namath's second book, *A Matter of Style* (with Bob Oates, Jr.), is an excellent study of professional football. It also offers an insight into Joe's own lifestyle—if the reader can separate the flipness from the facts.

Accounts of his personal life include details of his current pad — satin-sheeted oval bed, llama rug, gold bathroom fixtures, Italian marble bar, lavish pool table and game room. He also has homes in Florida, Alabama, and Pennsylvania, according to reports. True? Perhaps. Why shouldn't the boy from a steel town live it up as a celebrity?

Joe has been guided wisely by his attorney, James Walsh, and his business advisor, Mike Bite. Namath controls a chain of franchise restaurants, has set up an insurance agency for his two brothers, and has made other investments to insure a comfortable after-football future.

One project Joe doesn't talk about much is the Joe Namath Instructional Football Camp he runs in Dudley, Massachusetts. Yet every year, the star of the Jets mixes it up with young boys who may well be tomorrow's super players.

Joe Namath may always be a center of controversy and misunderstanding. Perhaps nobody will ever be able to separate the fact from the fiction.

It's said that Joe never uses public transportation. He rides around in limousines — claims they're cheaper in the long run in terms of time and trouble.

The title of his first book, *I Can't Wait Until Tomorrow,* is part of the old schoolboy clowning that finishes, "because I get better looking every day." Yet, some people insist, beneath the brash surface lurks a quiet man who is often shy with people and who doesn't usually seek the limelight.

Joe will shop for clothes in an army surplus store, laze around town in jeans and an old shirt, and then spend $500 on a tailored suit from Rome.

He's seen with glamorous girls from coast to coast, but saves his nicest compliments for those women who are least attractive.

He loves to travel and thinks nothing of boarding a plane to anywhere — just for dinner.

True?

False?

Man or myth? Maybe he doesn't know himself.

But Joe Namath, superstar, remains his own man. At ease anywhere and everywhere, with all kinds of people.

Whatever course his future may take, he'll still be unique. He may not have done much tackling in his football career, but it is a cinch he isn't afraid to tackle any future challenge —if he thinks it might be fun.